# Superpiss, Meltykiss, Spankers and Muff

# Superpiss, Meltykiss, Spankers and Muff

### Why some products will never make it in the English-speaking world

## GORDON THORBURN

CONSTABLE

Constable & Robinson Ltd
55-56 Russell Square
London WC1B 4HP

First published in the UK in 2012 by Constable,
an imprint of Constable & Robinson Ltd

A copy of the British Library Cataloguing in Publication Data is available from the British Library


ISBN 978-1-78033-901-6


Designed by Design 23, London
Printed in China

# CONTENTS

## AS WE WERE SAYING...

It's pronounced 'sheet-o', from the Ghanaian word for pepper, and the original is made of pepper and other spices ground up and fried in oil, to go with bland food such as fish. Unilever make a seasoning mix called Shito, same difference. More sophisticated versions actually contain fish, like dried shrimps. The cognoscenti may compare this to prawn ballichow.

Also in Ghana they have various other things ending in O, such as Nutso, a drink made from tiger nuts, and Boobo fruit juice.

These sex shoes are one-trip galoshes from China. Translations from the Chinese are invariably complex and subtle, and here the legend literally means 'ten thousand success set', but the word for set, tao, is also shorthand for condom in Taiwanese dialect, which, when you think about it, is a sort of galosh.

Rio BumBum is stuff for washing plates and so on in a dishwasher. If you are not completely satisfied, clip the coupon and complain.

A health drink that aptly replaces lost fluids and minerals in the body, it says here.

Indeed, Pocari Sweat is the most suitable drink for people going through dehydration because of everyday physical activities at work, in sports and at home, especially during summer. It has been Japan's favourite health drink since 1980.

The word Pocari doesn't mean anything, although it almost means wretched in Turkish, junk food in Romanian and sin in Spanish.

## Something Or Other

- SMOKE TURKEY DRUMSTICK
- SMOKE TURKEY WINGS
- SMOKE COW FEET
- COW SOMETHING

- FRESH PORK
- SALTED PIG FEET
- SALTED PIG TAIL
- FROZEN FISH

In the event of being unable to choose between smoke cow feet and salted pig tail, one can always lucky-dip with cow something.

## Gerber No More

*Avez vous gerbé du tout, à la mode de chez nous?* - as the old song almost went. Gerber baby food is not sold in UK, although it used to be, because that's the way owners Nestlé feel about it. The food is not sold in France either, possibly because gerber is the French verb to vomit.

## *These Foolish Mings*

The nearest we can get is mingherlino, meaning skinny or weedy, which surely cannot be the intention at this cafe in Florence near the Gallileo Museum. Mingin, innit.

# THE EARLY VILLAGE COCK

**'...hath twice done salutation to the morn,'**

as the Bard of Avon wrote entirely out of context, for we are dealing here with soup made of the cock in question.

We have to say that Audrey Baxter's version is rather tame, with its ingredients of leeks, rice, carrots and chicken, whereas Grace Kennedy of Jamaica, she who inhabits The Home of Caribbean Cuisine, also offers Fish Tea Soup – 'A delicious soup made from real fish' – and Mannish Water Ram Goat Soup. The latter is often served at weddings in the belief that its rather bolder chief ingredients, goat offal and green bananas, will better overcome shyness in the bridegroom than leeks and rice. And, as we all know, a cock can crow louder in its own farmyard.

# ESTONIAN GRAVY BROWNING

It's a shame but there's always a sensible explanation for things like this.

Kiek in de Kök is Estonian for Peep into the Kitchen, obviously, but what you may not have known is that it's the name given to a 15th century fortified tower in Talinn, so called because those manning the high ramparts said they could see down into the kitchens of the houses in the street.

Toompea is the seat of government, the old castle – sometimes called the Danish castle – that is their symbol of independence, last gained on August 20 1991. It is surely a word Tolkien could have used because Toompea doesn't mean anything in Estonian or, indeed, in that spelling, in any other European language except English.

We have a verb, not used much now, to toom, derived from the Old High German and Norse words for empty, as in 'Toom that pint down, lad, we're away'. The noun also means empty, in the sense of bereft, as in 'Will you still love me tomorrow, or will you leave me toom?' Or, Toompea is a village a few miles west of Hobbiton.

It could become a brand. Peep into the kitchen and you'll always find a packet of Toompea.

# SPOT THAT BRAND

The youth of today think they invented twittering tweets, but we know that it's only the technology that's new. People have twittered ever since they could, and here are a few examples from times past. Just to make it even more interesting, readers are invited to spot the brand names in the messages. There are nineteen altogether; answers on page 189.

**@ShakyBill**
Marlowe thou art of hind'ring knotgrass made. You are a noisy shit. Be gone.

**@BobLStevo**
Dear wife Fanny says I should rewrite *Treasure Island* with an extra parrot and more love juice, eg Scots serving wench Mary McPussy.

**@Errol_Flynn9**
Fancy a flirt, anyone? I'm high, gorgeous and ready to swashbuckle.

**@Marilyn362436**
Get lost, big nuts. I'd rather wack off Tarzan's cheetah. You've been around too long. Just burned meat.

**@Errol_Flynn9**
Hey, baby M. You still dating that wild drip of a play-writer? Come for lunch. I've got the ideal soup for sluts, but maybe you'd only puke.

**@Chairman_Mao**
Common ellol, Ellol. Snack pack look like Only Puke but name Only Pukeet. Dried beans with honey sweet coating.

**@Errol_Flynn9**
Thanks for that, Mr Chairman. May the sun bless your rice paddies.

**@Emperor_Hirohito**
May eggs of sacred crane be laid at your door.

**@Tobybelch**
Nips of whisky, gone arse over tit. Arse from elbow. Hic. Sandwich, anything. Open fridge. Unbelievable. This is not butter. Going for pee.

## ONE FOR HIS NOB

Noblice, Grom and Trick might well sound like a mid-European firm of solicitors, but they are sweetmeats made by the Serbian firm Banini at their factory in Belgrade. Noblice, as we can see, is a sort of choccy dodger. Grom is a choc wafer rather like KitKat, and Tricks are crackers which spur the consumer to complete enjoyment and make you feel the need to nibble it all day.

A similar need may be fulfilled at the annual Cattistock and Frome Valley Food Fest, in Dorset, where the Dorset Knob hand-made savoury biscuit is the centre of attention. According to local opinion, this very hard biscuit may indeed take you all day to nibble, unless you dip your Knob in cider or one of the beers from the Dorset Piddle brewery, such as Jimmy Riddle, Piddle bitter, or Cocky Hop.

The festival runs for most of the day and Knob Throwing is a major event, somewhat less taxing than the Highland Games where you would be tossing your caber with both hands. Here, you are only lobbing your Knob underarm. Besides Knob Throwing, there are additional fun knob attractions

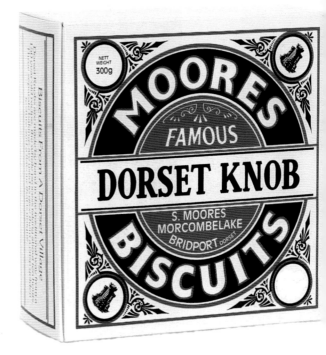

including Knob Eating, Knob Painting, a Knob and Spoon Race, Guess the Weight of the Big Knob, Knob Darts and a Knob Pyramid. Other, more traditional entertainment helps to make this a really enjoyable day out with a difference.

A knobber, incidentally, is a male deer in its second year, so to go knobbing is to hunt the stag.

# BEATING A PATH TO YOUR DOOR

According to Ralph Waldo Emerson, a better mousetrap will result in numerous gypsies offering to tarmac your drive, even if you live in the woods. Here is the proof.

Mouse-Land, made by the Taizhou Shenli Power Gum Development Co, comes with free poetry:

**Romantic rat night life.**
**The charming dashing habit is many.**
**Then the way fortune upons the strange monster.**
**Miserably and miserably and miserably I die.**

A sticky end indeed, while the Yi He Tuff Cat works more like the old-fashioned Little Nipper (illustrated).

**This model wooden trap is a most popular and easily operation. It is made of plastic.**
**They are largely used indoors and outside doors to kill or catch up different size of mice.**

Different size of mice get stuck in Euro Extra Mouse Glue, too.

**The product is safe, healthy and very ideal in wiping out rodents as there will be no chance of escape. Simply remove trapped mouse and re-use again.**

Ningbo Homart Houseware offers The Little Sucker, while Hangzhou Jiaxin Hardware makes a metal Nipper – perfect conqueror of guilty mouse – and a cage type trap:

**The product design is reasonable, the angle of the door is scientific. Also the dead rat will not smear the environment.**

# PORTABLE AT THE SAME TIME

In Korea, a few elderly men believe that eating dog increases abilities in the hanky-panky department, but businessfolk can see that this is not the way forward. A company called Easy for All makes DogCats Wipes.

**Usage: Cleans the mouth, ears, and feet of pets. After a pet's excretion.**

**To remove eye-wax of pets.**

**Features: Dogcats wipes quickly and easily use and portable at the same time. Dogcats wipes contains Sanicine, a material colorless, ordorless and without irritating effect, has been increasingly used throughout the world. Dogcats wipes ingredients sink well into the pet's skin that provides better disinfection.**

**Direction: Peel the seal attached on pouch (Do not remove it completely), and take out a sheet of wipe. Make sure reseal the tape after use for the remaining sheet to not to dry out.**

**Do not waste used sheet into the toilet bowl.**

They also make Baby Wipes, and Toothcleaner Wipes:

**Tooth cleaner combined with dental floss. Can clean teeth without water. Being portable, it can be conveniently used anywhere and at any time. Designed to cover your mouth with the cleansing wipe to avoid causing a revulsion from sights and smells.**

We are warned not to use the Multi-Purpose Wipes on cycle seats, as the slippery ingredient may cause an accident.

McVitie's ®

# HobnObs

✓ No artificial
colours or flavours

✓ 45% Oat
and Wholemeal

**DARK CHOC** NOBBLY OATY BISCUITS

| Calories | Sugars | Fat | Saturates | Salt |
|----------|--------|------|-----------|------|
| 95 | 6.0g | 4.6g | 2.3g | 0.2g |
| 5% | 7% | 7% | 12% | 3% |

# A BRAND IS BORN

Biscuits tend to have generic names – bourbon, custard cream, digestive – and supermarket chains will always make their own-label versions to compete with the  brands. As supermarkets are also the biscuit brands' biggest customers, there is bound to be a difficulty every time a new biscuit is invented.

The brief from McVitie's to their branding consultants, when this oat crunch knobbly biscuit was developed, was to try and give it a name which was protectable, to an extent, but didn't overshadow the maker's name. Consumer tests were so positive that a really strong name was clearly needed and so, by a process known only to the creative genii in the branding firm, Hobnobs was decided upon.

The name had various warm and cuddly associations but, more importantly, it could be registered and protected, and very good they are too, especially the chocolate coated ones.

Hob-nobbing used to be hab-nabbing, from 'Hab or Nab', hit or miss, have or have not, which gradually came to be associated with drinking partners offering each other toasts, and so to being on friendly terms. Have a Hobnob. Why, thank you.

## B. K. MILLER
## Meats and Liquors, Inc.

| | |
|---|---|
| **Fresh Lump Crap Meat** <br> 1 LB CUP | $9.95 EA |
| **Whiting or Trout Fillets** <br> 10 LB SHEET | $16.95 EA |
| **Snow Crab Leg Clusters** <br> 2 LB BOX | $10.95 EA |
| **Fresh Chicken Drumsticks** <br> 40 LB BOX | $15.95 BX |
| **Fresh Chicken Wings** <br> 40 LB BOX | $45.95 BX |
| **Assorted Pork Chops** <br> FAMILY PACKS | $1.79 LB |
| **Miller Genuine Draft, or Lite** <br> EVERYDAY PRICE     30 PACK CANS | $16.99 EA |

WE SELL ICE MELTERS BY THE BAG OR PALLET

## Something Fishy . . .

Fresh and lumpy, but is it crab or crap? This great American shop also offers ice melters by the bag – we just warm up ice at home by putting it in a G&T – and Miller (no relation) genuine draught beer but in tins.

## The Big Issue

Here we are in Denmark, where they make a salt-liquorice pastille called saltlakrid, apparently an acquired taste, and a wine gum version, vinnigummi, which is more the usual thing.

## Pucker Up

Meltykiss is a range of cubic chocolates, including green tea flavour, made by the Meiji Company of Tokyo. They offer many other chocolatey manifestations including chocolate letters, like type but the right way round, that you can set into a soppy message for Valentine's Day (yes, they have it in Japan too). They also make pharmaceuticals, notably at the Dong Myung factory in Korea, and are dedicated to brightening their customers' daily lives through food and health. Or, to put it another way, they will leverage the corporate merger to broaden their business domain.

# THE BRAND THAT WILL NOT DIE

There's an old *Punch* cartoon that has a fellow asking the waiter if what he has is coffee, in which case he'd like tea, but if it's tea, he'd like coffee. Bearing in mind the majority British attitude to and knowledge of coffee until really quite recently, the cartoon was right on the button.

In the early 1960s, your correspondent's mother's idea of a coffee was a spoonful of Camp in a cup of hot milk, while her son knew that a coffee newly came out of a steaming, shiny steel machine, was served in a wide-brimmed Pyrex cup with a lot of froth on the top, and cost nine old pence in the Cat's Whisker Coffee Bar.

Back in 1876, unconfirmed legend has it that the Glasgow firm of Paterson and Sons was asked by the Gordon Highlanders to develop a quick coffee that could be served up easily on campaign. That would have seemed like a fairly limited market - we were fighting the Zulu Wars by then – but if an instant coffee-style drink was to be a hit with the public, there were some serious difficulties to be overcome.

It was a time when everybody drank tea. Coffee was expensive and too complex to make properly if you had no servants, and so Paterson's product was largely chicory, much cheaper, and it was sold on it being ready, always ready – so instant and convenient, in fact, that it could be had while camping.

To overcome market resistance – very few Glaswegians went camping and, as we say, coffee was generally unknown – they put a Scottish soldier on the label, an officer of the Gordon Highlanders, with a Sikh servant standing by with tray, bottle and jug. The label said it was coffee with chicory, although it had hardly any coffee in it, and the advertising slogan said it was made of High Grade Coffee by Coffee Experts.

In modern times the Sikh was shown without his tray and since 2006, much to the dismay of the *Daily Mail*, he has sat with the officer, whose tartan pattern and furry bonnet have been much simplified to anonymity, and who has grown younger with a smaller moustache. There is no second tent in the background and no sword on the ground. The logo has been redrawn – it was just simple lettering in inverted commas – and the two men drink the stuff together, a concession to post-imperial political correctness or, according to the makers, a case of continual development after careful consideration.

What if the brand were being launched now? Camp has acquired an extra and entirely different meaning, especially where a man in a skirt is involved, and people can choose from a hundred different brands of instant coffee that are actually made of coffee, rather than one that admits to 26% chicory, 4% coffee, with the other 70% being sugar and water.

It mostly goes in cakes and other confections – great to use in baking, it says – and it's still selling, but we have to say that, were it not for its already being there, it wouldn't be there.

# NICE ONE, CYRIL

Every English speaking child, on first encountering these biscuits, thinks to himself, 'I thought all biscuits were supposed to be nice.'

They are made by most biscuit manufacturers and have been for a century or more, they are pleasant to the taste if you like coconut, and there is unresolved disagreement about whether they are nice or from Nice.

Huntley and Palmer made a version in 1904, from flour, sugar, butter, coconut, milk, vanilla and baking soda. Our modern one pictured, from the Co-op, has palm oil instead of butter.

Eastman Industries of Ludhiana in the Punjab also make them, while aspiring to improve the value, wealth and well-being of its stakeholders, thereby becoming the most preferred supplier in every country they operate in, by 'offering top-quality, value-for-money products made possible through aggressive sourcing quality products and cutting inefficiencies in value chain.'

# FISHERMEN'S FRIENDS

It may be news to many but, according to the blurb on the label, Fishshot is today probably the most popular shot in the world.

> **The refreshing taste of Fishshot is made from a secret blend including eucalyptus, menthol, liquorice and premium vodka. Many have without luck tried to imitate this unique recipe, which is only known by the family owners.**

They certainly like their liquorice up there in Viking land (see Spunk, page 30). The ingredients, we can see, apart from the vodka, are the same as in Nigroids tablets, now called Vigroids, which 'protect the breathing apparatus from the foggy foggy dew, and in Fisherman's Friend lozenges, which were first made to give chesty comfort on the high seas.'

ORIGINAL
# Seaman's Shot
## extra hot

Seaman's Shot extra hot, is a combination
of the finest triple distilled vodka and
natural flavours of menthol, eucalyptus
and liquorice. Enjoy Seaman's Shot
extra hot at room temperature, chilled
on its own or with a beer.

### With Vodka

Extra hot - Extra refreshing - Shake well before pouring

ORIGINAL
# Seaman's Shot
## cool lemon

Seaman's Shot cool lemon, is a
combination of the finest triple distilled
vodka and natural flavours of menthol
and lemon. Enjoy Seaman's Shot
cool lemon at room temperature,
chilled, on its own or with a beer.

### with vodka

Extra hot - Extra refreshing - Shake well before pouring

ORIGINAL
## eaman's
## Shot
## xtra hot

Seaman's Shot extra hot, is a combination
of the finest triple distilled vodka and
natural flavours of menthol, eucalyptus
and liquorice. Enjoy Seaman's Shot

This must explain the fishy, sea-going connection in the branding of these drinks. Ploughman's Shot? Bank Manager's Shot? Doesn't work, somehow.

So, you have a tea-clipper as the logo on one brand, and a morose trawler man on the other who doesn't seem to want you to have any.

However, you are enjoined to drink Seaman's Shot Extra Hot, same ingredients, chilled on its own or with a beer. It's German but made, we feel, with or without luck, for the Scandinavian market.

The Zubes that we knew when sweets were rationed, are no longer, and they never did contain liquorice. Still, they were soothing, warm and pleasant, like a Seaman's Shot, the addition to which of Zubes' Balsam of Tolu would also stop that tickling cough.

## ZUBES ARE BEST FOR THROAT AND CHEST

Beware of Old Man Winter's cold, clammy claws! Rain, frost and fog can soon cause husky, sore throats and wheezy chests. Give yourself the protection of soothing, warming, pleasant Zubes — they simply can't be beaten! Zubes are scientifically prepared — contain Balsam of Tolu to *stop tickling coughs*, Menthol to *ease catarrh*, Ginger and Capsicum to *warm you*, and Peppermint and Aniseed to *soothe your throat and chest*. This winter — go suck a Zube! Go buy a tin — today! 5½d. an oz. loose; and in 8½d. and 1/4d. tins.

# Hoarse? go suck a

# ZUBE

*Zubes Cough Mixture containing the famous Zubes ingredients, 1/7d. and 2/11d.*

# THE INFLUENCE OF HARLOTS

Pornography, as a word, is a fairly recent usage. Before the mid-19th century, we had to use other terms but then the French came in with *le pornographe*, one who describes the lives and manners of prostitutes and their patrons. We should admire the forward-thinking French, for this was long before the invention of the phonograph, the cinematograph and the *Daily Telegraph*.

It's all to do with the Greek for harlot and, seizing on the French innovation, British historians were quick to coin a term for the governance of Rome in the first half of the tenth century.

Yes, you guessed it, pornocracy – the dominating influence of harlots – was the name given to the time when Senatrix Theodora and her daughters, Marozia and Theodora Junior, more or less ruled Rome. Their leadership of the nobility was characterised by corruption, licentiousness and all manner of how's your father, between (roughly) 900 and 930 AD.

Marozia is especially interesting as she had popes in more than one sense. Pope Sergius III is supposed to have fathered her firstborn when she was only fifteen, which baby went on to become a pope himself, John XI, after his mum imprisoned the current one, Stephen VII, and probably had him murdered.

Thailand and porn are no strangers, we know, and so we must question the common sense of the Bangkok manufacturers of children's clothes who decided on Porn as their brand name.

## PimPim, Bob and Bong

Swedish corner shops also have PimPim jelly boats, Juleskum - a kind of marshmallow, Pigall - like a Milky Bar, Kex chocolate, and Pucko drinking chocolate. Bob, Festis and Onos are all soft drinks and, on the healthy side, you must have some God Morgon Gruel to give you a moment of warmth and pleasure for both body and soul. If you change your mind, you might like Abba Fishballs, perhaps with some Slotts Mustard, and there's always Bong fish stock.

## More Spankers, Vicar?

Delicious syrup cake with lots of rum butter, made in Holland, is only one of the world's Spankers. The others – Baby Spankers, Senior Spankers and Hotlips Spankers for instance – are, rather disappointingly, big-game fishing lures from Maryland, USA.

# THE MAGICAL WORLD OF PRODUCT PLACEMENT

A great deal of media coverage and discussion among the chattering classes has been devoted to product placement as a way of funding TV shows. In America it seems like second nature. You expect to see Coca Cola and Starbucks during *Sex in the City*, but what is British television doing about it?

We can expect new series of *Downton Abbey* to carry on for ever, provided they can offset the huge costs of costumes for a thousand actors in five hundred simultaneous mini-plots. Placing contemporary British brands in the script must be an option, especially names that might seem amusing to eager viewers in the USA, not to mention the Countess of Grantham, the multi-squillionaire American who is herself one of the smartest ever examples of product placement. Imagine the scene. It's tea time at the Abbey.

**Lord G:**
(to maid, putting down tea tray)    Ah, Jane, thank you. Robertson's strawberry jam. My favourite. Have we collected enough labels for our enamel gollywog badge?

| | |
|---|---|
| **Lady G:** | Really, darling, you are so childish. Pass me a mince pie, would you? |
| **Lord G:** | Robertson's mincemeat, no doubt. One step nearer my enamel badge. I think I'll have a biscuit. Have you tried M and D's Crax? |
| **Lady G:** | I prefer McVitie and Price's Ginger Nuts. |
| **Lord G:** | Or their Hobnobs. I realise Hobnobs haven't been invented yet but we don't mind anachronisms at *Downton Abbey*. By the way, has the car come back yet from the garage? |
| **Lady G:** | No, it hasn't. I telephoned Cockshoots myself and they said we should never have |

put Benzole in it. I blame the chauffeur. He's always fiddling with his Screwmaster. His mind isn't on the job.

**Lord G:** And then there's the perambulator for the grandson. Nanny recommended an English Queen, but I'm not sure that will give the boy the best start in life. What do you prefer, my dear? Are you happy to take a Swallow?

**Lady G:** I should say the same to any girl, of our class or not. Swallow, most definitely, for all the advantages of a drop-end pramette.

(Lord G reaches for his pipe) And darling, I do wish you wouldn't smoke in the drawing room. What's that tobacco? It's not that awful stuff, Three Nuns?

**Lord G:** Nearly right, dear. Churchman's Shag. I thought Lady Mary looked rather unhappy at dinner.

**Lady G:** Yes, she did not have her usual gracious expression of personality. I have recommended a new perfume. Lady Gay.

**Lord G:** Really? Lady Gay? Is everything all right between Lady Mary and Matthew?

**Lady G:** Certainly. The moment he was out of his wheelchair, he was off to Prickard to order his tail suit for the wedding...

And what could be done with *Silent Witness?*

**Harry:** It seems to me that this woman, whose body we are showing naked for medical reasons, has been on holiday.

**Nikki:** Oh, Harry, you're so wonderful. How can you tell? Love the designer stubble, by the way. Hope it won't get more close-ups than my great big googly eyes.

**Harry:** I can tell, Nikki, by the residue of Mukki brand extra-digestible milk in her duodenum. This can only mean one thing. And yes, I am too good looking to be a pathologist. Maybe I'll be the next James Bond.

**Nikki:** What? You're too good looking? What about me? You should see me walk away from camera. Anyway, what only thing can it mean?

**Harry:** That she's been to Italy, Nikki, where they have Mukki, all kinds of Mukki brand milk products, including yoghurt.

**Nikki:** Mukki brand yoghurt? Is it available all over Italy?

**Harry:** Unfortunately, although it's made from the freshest and purest Tuscan milk, it is available all over Italy, so I can't tell exactly where she's been.

**Nikki:** What about the cause of death, Harry?

| | |
|---|---|
| **Harry:** | First we must answer the question, 'Why would she drink washing-up liquid?' |
| **Nikki:** | Italian washing-up liquid? You must mean Rio Bum Bum. Con glicerina. |
| **Harry:** | Precisely. My guess is that she couldn't speak Italian, and so mistook it for pink grapefruit juice. |
| (Enter Leo) | |
| **Nikki:** | Oh, Leo, there you are at last. Come over here. Harry's so clever. He's discovered Mukki and Bum Bum in the murder victim. |
| **Leo:** | Sorry I'm late. Just got back from Sweden. Too much pickled herring. Got a touch of the runs. Luckily, there was plenty of Kiss Me brand loo paper on the aeroplane. |
| **Nikki:** | I prefer the Japanese one, called Pity. Really soft and gentle on my gorgeous rear end, which you can admire in my walking-away-from-camera shots. |
| **Harry:** | Look, chaps, must get on. I'm out tonight for a Chinese meal. New branch of the My Dung restaurant chain's opened up near me. |
| **Nikki:** | My Dung? Oh, Harry. I love My Dung. |

## WAKE UP WITH A START

The Czech cigarette Start, now made by Philip Morris, used to be the equivalent of yellow Gauloise or Park Drive in marketing terms. They were the working man's tab, cheap, with free bits of wood among the baccy, a baptism of fire for Czech youngsters who would emulate their elders. Any such tyro sticking with cigarettes after starting on Start was a real man.

It is disappointing to find that the obscure-seeming words on the packet, with all those strange accents, translate thus.

**The Ministry of Health warns that Smokers die prematurely.
Smoking seriously harms you and the people around you.**

There is no word 'start' in Czech, but it was adopted from English by the Russians in the 1950s/60s to mean the launching of a spacecraft, and so probably this is where the cigarette got its name. The only other manifestation of start in Czecho is on PC screens as an icon you need to click if you want to stop.

## MAY CONTAIN NUTS

Most of the amusing messages on packages derive from company lawyers afraid of being sued – 'Do not use as a hair drier' on a blowtorch, 'Mouse may contain wool', that sort of thing.

For more imaginative legends, we must turn to the Far East. Sweet Dream, for example, is rather a nice brand name for cake, but it is the copy on the pack which is really attractive.

**This cake is very savory! How is teatime at everybody? The cake which my mama burned is what is more delicious than the cake of the store of the throat in the world. Therefore, daily teatime enjoys itself very much and it is!**

You have to admire the comma after 'Therefore', but you might prefer an apple pie to a cake.

> **Each apple has been brought up carefully like his own baby by farmers in the village of apples. They are all crimson and very cheerful now. Putting it into your mouth, its sweetness and moderate sourness are wonderful. You must feel just like biting fresh nature itself. Please relish these pies which we baked, making much of such apples' feelings. That is sure to fill you with a fresh taste.**

Each apple has been brought up carefully like his own baby by farmers in the village of apples. They are all crimson and very cheerful now. Putting it into your mouth, its sweetness and moderate sourness are wonderful. You must feel just like biting fresh nature itself. Please relish these pies which we baked, making much of such apples' feelings. That is sure to fill you with a fresh taste.

This is more literate English than a great many native speakers could manage, including the apostrophe when alluding to the feelings of apples. It's more evocative and graceful than the work of many modern poets. So, who are we to mock?

# *ME AND YOU AND A BOY TOY NAMED CHOU*

Almost everybody likes Chinese food. Readers of a certain age will remember the surprise and delight of those restaurants suddenly springing up everywhere in the late 1950s and early 60s. Before there were any Indian restaurants in ordinary high streets, or Thai, or anything like that, we could spend six shillings to marvel at food we had never seen before: chicken and sweetcorn soup, a semi-translucent bowl of blandness for which the word 'glutinous' might have been coined; balls of batter with tiny cubes of pork inside, drowned in a vinegary, lurid, red-orange sauce, the antecedents of which we could not even guess at; and bits of fruit in a whitish kind of toffee coating that the socially neutral waiter dropped into cold water, to be served with transparent custard.

Your correspondent's own initiation was in London aged 15, after visiting the 1961 Motor Show at Earls Court with parents, where were shown the very lovely E-Type Jag and the less than lovely Mark X. Quite how the comestibly conservative guardians came to visit such a novelty as a Chinese restaurant we cannot tell, but the memory of chicken chow mein with crispy noodles lives on.

We thought we were being wildly, orientally, adventurous. Now we know different. We know that Vesta chop suey was not actually what the Chinese ate nor, for that matter, was number 63 Special Fried Rice.

We know that you need more than a wok and some

| | Soups | | | |
|---|---|---|---|---|
| 罗 | 宋 | 汤 | | *The soup of Sung* |
| 粟 | 米 | 汤 | | *Maize soup* |
| 周 | 打 | 鱼 | 汤 | *The week beats the fish soup* |
| 牛 | 尾 | 浓 | 汤 | *Thick soup in oxtail* |
| 鸡 | 耳 | 忌 | 廉 汤 | *The chicken hates the soup of* |

soy sauce to produce 'Eight-fingernail Fish', not to mention 'Fires an Employee Spicily the Head', the way in which a certain menu offered a dish of octopus tentacles with plenty of fresh chillies or, as they say in Beijing, 'the beautiful woman peppers.'

'Old Nominal Mother stir Friend Kidneys' is really quick and easy to make if you can find the ingredients, but we must ask ourselves if it's worth going to any trouble at all to cook 'Stir-fry Cattle River with No Result.' No need to set the timer when you're cooking 'The Palace Oil Explodes the Duck', but be careful whom you invite to dinner if you are going to serve 'Black Chicken with Drug.'

So, if you happen to be in China and are not a Chinese speaker, you must remember, before giving vent to hilariousness, that written Chinese consists of characters that are monosyllabic. When combined with other characters to form compound words or phrases, they can evolve into something else, with further complications resulting from the different ways they can be pronounced.

So, you may be deeply disappointed to find that 'The Soup of Sung' is not an ancient dish from Foochow named for a great hero, who invented it after slaying a thousand barbarians, nor is it, despite the hints in the Chinese characters, actually from the time of the imperial Sung dynasty, an era of great sophistication.

It is not like Sung Hua Jou, indeed from Foochow, which is pine-flower meat soufflé omelette (according to Kenneth Lo, although there is no pine flower in his recipe), nor is it like Sung Shu Yü, a deep-fried dish called squirrel fish, allegedly for the squirrel-chatter noise it makes when the sauce is poured over. Sung in that case is a different character altogether from the one with the soup of Sung, but with a very similar sound, being the first syllable of the word for squirrel and of the word for pine. Confused? It's not over yet.

No, 'The Soup of Sung' is none of these. It is, in fact, borscht, or Russian soup, and we are looking at a menu of western dishes, possibly not served in the restaurant pictured. The names in English have been translated into Chinese characters, then back into the English whence they came, suffering from the famous Chinese whispers on the way.

'Russian' transliterates into characters approximately representing the sounds Lou Sung, because Chinese does not have the R sound and people have difficulty saying it, hence the famous flied lice. Ferrari is impossible but, fortuitously, the transliteration fa la li means something like 'magic weapon pull power.'

The Japanese are, of course, the other way round and say gorofu instead of golf. Anyway, when the menu chap was confronted with lou sung, he didn't think 'Ah, Lussian,' but translated it literally as 'luxurious sung', which he thought must mean the Emperor Sung, and so there you are.

'The Week Beats the Fish Soup' comes from an attempt to render the word 'chowder', using characters representing the sounds zhou da. Our diligent menuist, confronted with same, knows not of chowder but does know that those

two Chinese characters basically mean 'week beat' and, despite the odd collocation, draws the obvious conclusion for this weird food eaten by foreigners.

Some of them are easy to fathom. 'Maize' is sweet corn, and 'thick soup in oxtail' simply has it the wrong way about.

'The Chicken Hates the Soup' because it has mushrooms in it, possibly. The characters roughly mean that the confused, fluffy or luxuriant growth chicken is disgusted by or is complaining about the soup. 'Luxuriant growth' in this context probably means fungus which, as it is a western dish, comes out as chicken and mushroom. Anyone thinking of learning Chinese should bear this sort of thing in mind.

And for your next course, you will be pleased to know, you can choose from 'Pastoral Salad' and 'Swallow to Take the Fish Salad', rather than sand.

We must imagine that, all over China, the restaurant owners' Number One sons are possessed of a Chinese-English dictionary and a poetical spirit, but little knowledge of your actual English. How else can we explain 'Dried Ball Bursts into Rage (braise in soy sauce, burnt sneak away)'? Next time you're in the supermarket, looking at ready-cut porky bits for yet another stir-fry, think of 'The Peasant Family

| Fuck the pot, bao zhai, water to boil the type | |
| --- | --- |
| 干锅鱼头 | Fuck a fish head |
| 锅仔双冬肚分 | Pot zhai double dong belly |
| 干锅童子鸡 | Fuck a spring chicken |
| 干锅墨鱼仔 | Fuck a cuttlefish zhai |
| 巴渝酸菜鱼 | Ba yu sour pickled cabbage fish |
| 干锅牛蛙 | Fuck a bullfrog |
| 干锅腊肉茶树菇 | Fuck a la meat tea tree the gu |

stir-fries Flesh for a Short Time', and all will seem slightly less boring.

So, get cooking, but not with a bottle of sweet-and-sour like our take-aways. Go for the real thing. Mind you, 'Double Dong Belly' could be a problem. The only polite dongs we know are the ones that go with dings, and the ones that have luminous noses and wander through the forest at midnight. It is no help to know that donga is Bantu for a steep-sided ravine.

The double-dong menu is of proper Chinese dishes and the explanation is simple. The Chinese character kan (first on the left for fish head, spring chicken etc) is a crude colloquial term for having sex, but more politely it means dry, as in that form of cooking not unlike sauté. Our translator obviously didn't know any French but knew some plain English.

Thus we have fish head sauté in a pot, and pork belly slices double boiled with winter melon in a small pot, which is to say poached in a double boiler or bain Marie, rather than plain boiled twice over. We also have sauté spring chicken in a pot and sauté baby cuttlefish in a pot.

'Ba yu' possibly is the restaurant name, as in chef's special pickled cabbage with fish, then there's sauté bullfrog in a pot, and sauté waxed meat with tea-tree mushroom. This last is a seasonal delicacy;

pork is smoked and wrapped in wax to preserve it, hung out to dry and eaten during winter.

Choosing from the short menu is somewhat easier. 'Stems' are sprouts, as in bean sprouts, and 'boy toy' is neither an inappropriate romantic liaison nor a computer game called Garrotte the Naked Policewoman 4. It is merely a misspelling of bak choi, or mustard greens.

With that sorted, you can pop into the Chinese supermarket, have a look at the brands on the shelves and let your dining imagination run free. There's a soft drink your guests will appreciate, called Red Date, which is portable, can

improve human immunity and, if you drink of it often, you will look more beautiful and younger. To finish the meal, give your guests some Ailesi Poke Chinese chocolate, wrapped in a simulated 200 Euro note, or Korea Stone chocolate from the Acme Fate Co of Qingdao, or perhaps one of Mr Fang's 'natural Synthetic Handmade Cookies', with 'taste coming from nature', always remembering that cookie in Hungarian (kuki) means penis.

## That Takes The Biscuit

These resimli (illustrated), bisküi are called Bum! because such is the word in Turkish for pop, as in balloon. Or, as in the song: 'That's the way the money goes, Bum! goes the sansar.'

# MOTHER'S DAY

In America they have Mum-Mum baby snacks (or Snax). In Australia there is Yum Mum Gourmet Organic baby food. Nevertheless, Egypt is really the place for Mummy or, in this case, Mom.

Egyptian Mom's Food includes Relax herbal drinks, bringing you the strengthening and immunity discovered in herbs by the Ancient Egyptians. Likewise, Mom's Food Palm Date Preserve 'is your opportunity to surprise anyone who thinks he or she has seen it all in the world of preserves.'

Such people are everywhere these days. World of preserves? Seen it all, mate. Ah but, you can say, what about the chutneys? These are good too, because Mom learned the secret of Traditional Indian Chutney from the wife of her family butler and, as we can see from the picture, wrote down the recipe.

You want soup? Let's Soup is Mom's soup-in-a-jar. Just heat one and eat it in less than two minutes.

If you have time after that, try some Shata cheese or, from the Promo Speed company, 'canilony' and 'overstuffed mmbar.'

Being in Egypt, you will not be surprised to find Cleopatra lollipops and Sandy fruit sweets, or Tattoo chewing gum come to that.

Herbal medicine can be mystifying, and nowhere more so than in the land of the pharaohs. How about 'Bride for Lapping Cream Skin'? Or, take Snello, 'a herbal slimming powder that increases fecal bulk.' Or, for a mother's day treat, there's Willy Cream and Al-Omare Herbal Delayer – 'a cream consisting of bee wax and the delaying herb, a tiny piece should be applied to the male organ and left an hour then washed with warm water.'

Phew. After all that, you may be attracted by Pillow Small Chillout Pufs, but be warned. They can be used to watch movies or to wrestle.

# DO NOT WANT HEAVY FALL

Chinese cooks don't use a wok for everything. When the persons eating are also the cooks, in a form of fondue called Shua, there is a special pot for it, sometimes called a firepot, traditionally made of brass or other metal but, in today's more fashionable homes, it could be glass.

The firepot can be used with broth or plain water for seething, or oil for frying. In the former case, the by-product is a subtly flavoured soup with which you end the meal.

Now, read the instructions carefully before setting said pot on your table, in front of dinner guests equipped with dried fish, slivers of Mongolian lamb, chopsticks and little saucers of dips.

1. **Please don't will just burn hot oil direct pour into pot of in, for fear result in glass pot of body of because temperature rapid change but rupture.**
2. **Pot of as glass, please don't with other hard thing collision, do not want heavy fall.**
3. **Please don't will fill oily oilcan put flaring cooking range beside, for fear mouth of a jug be heated distortion.**
4. **Oilcan at clean in process, do not want use steel wires ball games de clean Shua for fear scrape spend oilcan affect beautiful.**

Chopstick fumblers dropping their morsels into the hot oil must not swear or curse, but rather 'let the elegant flower fragrance accompany you together with your heart in the whole poetic afternoon.'

¥460

¥250

## SUSHI OR NOT SUSHI?

Japan is a fruitful hunting ground for brand oddities and many other kinds of fractured English. This is partly because Japanese and English have so little in common as languages, and partly because Japan has been so closely involved with America for so long – yet they never seem to ask a native English speaker to check their material.

What could they have been thinking of, when they decided on Skinababe as a name for a baby cream? Also in the drugstore, you'll find Cat Wetty moistened hand-wipes, Blow Up hairspray, Dessert toothpaste and My Fannie kitchen roll.

Infected with the same diet madness that spins money in the western world, the Japanese have come up with Jesus Body diet pills containing Ultrasome®. Whatever Ultrasome might be chemically, it's a bit of a breakthrough.

> **New discovery to be kept from others. This discovery is a secret. I can lay it down because I am correct. We will not make you sorry. Pleasure to have the real thing. I really longed for this.**

You can see what he's getting at. It's new. It's true. It works. It's what you always wanted. It does exactly what it says on the packet as, possibly, does the liquid inside the Perfect Eye Remover bottle, or the nose beauty tool called Nose Up, or the Scratch Picky Magic 3-in-1 Blackhead Remover Tool.

Further down the high street is a minimart grocery. A loaf of bread? Hmm, not really a Japanese thing, but you could try Germ brand. There's also I'm Dripper instant coffee, if you'd

NIKKA

prefer that to Straight Tea, in which case, unless you take your I'm Dripper black, you will surely want some Creamy Powder, abbreviated as Creap.

After a quick look around the hardware shop, where they stock cock heaters, you might like to cool off with a nice fruity milk drink such as Calpis*, but mind you don't spill any on your Trim Pecker trousers. Or you could take something stronger, like Black Nikka whisky, with the King of Blenders on the label as a vaguely Scottish version of Henry VIII.

What? You haven't bought anything? Oh no, you must.

> **These products are gathered with taste. When we sell this commodity, the store manager rejoices. It is rapture. Consider the mental welfare of our employees and please buy this commodity.**

*It's basically a low-fat sweetened yoghurt with fruit flavour added. Here is India's answer to Nigella, Madhur Jaffrey, writing in 1980 with a perfectly straight face:

> **Japan, which has almost no tradition of consuming milk products, has come up with a new drink that is likely to prove very popular. It is called Calpis and is sold (in the USA) under the name Calpico.**

# THE CUP THAT CHEERS

Sake is normally served in little porcelain cups, so it makes sense to pack it in one-cup size: Fukucup 200.

The ancient Fukumitsuya brewery, in the town of Kanazawa on the western coast of Honshu, makes many varieties of Junmai sake.

**Rich in rice flavours and leave pleasant after-taste, and also make a great company with dishes. This is the taste we have been pursuing. Our skilled brewers listen to what nature provides and understand what to do. This process can never be replaced by machine.**

A message there, perhaps for some of the larger brewers on this side of the world.

The main ingredients are water and rice – special varieties of rice and special water, called hyakunensui.

**Hyakunensui, one-hundred-year-old water in English and water used to brew our sakes, begins as rain and snow falling at the foot of the Mount Hakusan. This water spends at least 100 years slowly filtering through deep underground. It then reaches the well of our brewery, blessed with minerals that are necessary for fermentation. We thank the wonder of nature everyday.**

Another message for our major brewers, and that's not the end of it. They make one called Momotose, much aged, that has an 'elegant and mature flavour that you have never experienced', and finally we have sake for Smooth Tender Skin.

**Sake is not only a drink, also a beauty aid. Geishas have used sake as a facial lotion before putting on makeup. It is a famous story that sake brewery workers have beautiful, clear hands. It is great for those who experience skin irritation from alcohol, since it contains no alcohol.**

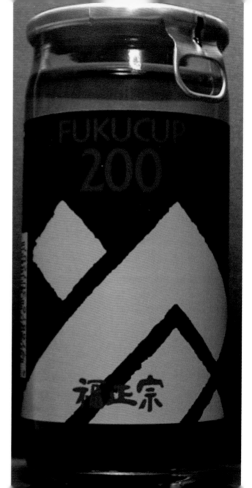

# IN THE PUB

*Good cocktails begin with cold Fart,*
*And Fockink liqueur. Plus one part*
*Of lemonish Zit*
*And a dollop of Pshitt,*
*To serve in a cup of Hot Art.*

Fart is a Polish brand of fruit juice; sokow is juice, and fart translates approximately as luck, as in happy accident or fluke.

Wynand Fockink is a fine old Dutch distilling firm, making a wide range of liqueurs and jenevers. Zit is a Greek soft drink made with lemons and limes, and Pshitt is, or was, a similar thing in France, but famously orange.

The drinking vessel is a bit of poetic licence, being a Japanese brand of paper cup called The Art of Hot, which the manufacturers turn into an irresistible purchase with the lines:

**Side by side I'll be yours forever.**
**Because please don't weep.**

If you are in the mood for weeping, a swig of Looza, the Belgian fruit juice, might make you feel better. You can get it in many countries, including the USA, where one supplier says:

**If you have not try any of our Looza Juices**
**do not missed out.**

And that's in America, where they speak English most of the time.

Thank you for
**NO OUTSIDE
FOOD/ DRINK!**

THE **CREAM PUFF**

ビア★パパ

作りたてシュークリーム専門店

Beard Papa's fresh'n natural cream puffs. We are constantly
striving towards freshness & homemade taste by carefully
choosing each and every ingredient that goes into our
products. In consideration of your health, no additives or
preservatives are used.

BEARD PAPA'S WORLDWIDE CHAINS: JAPAN, USA, UK, AUSTRALIA, KOREA, TAIW
HONG KONG, SINGAPORE, MALAYSIA, PH
THAILAND, INDONESIA :

Segar

Please Pay at Cashier
Thank You ☺

## SEX IN THE CAFE

It is very unlikely, should you visit the Cream Puff Cafe in Kuala Lumpur, or any other cafe for that matter, that you will be able to put a splash of Bra milk in your Hardon tea. The reasons for this are manifold, the chief one for the milk being that the Swedish company that makes it has gone all po-faced global and renamed it as Natur.

Such spoilsporting does not apply to the United Sugar Trading Company NV, based in Curaçao in the former Dutch Antilles, which proudly markets Hardon black tea wherever Dutch is spoken, and elsewhere. As their PR puts it:

**With the use of our production of high standard we have established a proper market; we are specialized in advising our clients in the development of "Private Labeling".**

We manufacture and mix miscellaneous basic raw material for the food industry in the Dutch Antilles and Europe.

Our mission is to add vitality to life. We meet everyday needs for nutrition, that help people feel good, look good and get more out of life. We try to satisfy completely the expectations of our clients by means of manufacturing, distribution and the commercialization of tea and sugar of high quality.

Our Vission: We are a company with added value and which takes part in the commercialization and distribution of products as the tea and the sugar on the national and international markets.

And you can't say fairer than that.

# Hardon Tea

## 100 Class A

## Teabags

Ingredients: 100% Tea

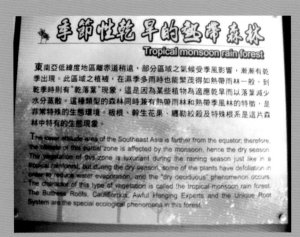

東南亞低緯度地區離赤道稍遠，部分區域之氣候受季風影響，漸漸有乾季出現。此區域之植被，在濕季多雨時也能繁茂得如熱帶雨林一般，到乾季時則有"乾落葉"現象，這是因為某些植物為適應乾旱而以落葉減少水分蒸散。這種類型的森林同時兼有熱帶雨林和熱帶季風林的特徵，是非常特殊的生態環境。板根、幹生花果、纏勒絞殺及特殊根系是這片森林中特有的生態現象。

The lower altitude area of the Southeast Asia is farther from the equator; therefore, the climate of this partial zone is affected by the monsoon, hence the dry season. The vegetation of this zone is luxuriant during the raining season just like in a tropical rainforest, but during the dry season, some of the plants have defoliation in order to reduce water evaporation, and the "dry deciduous" phenomenon occurs. The character of this type of vegetation is called the tropical monsoon rain forest. The Buttress Roots, Cauliflorous, Awful Hanging Experts and the Unique Root System are the special ecological phenomena in this forest.

**BEAVER CLEANERS**

(416) 781-6747      3693

## Hang The Experts

It's green, they say, on the far side of the hill, and the exigencies of global warming are not always apparent to the traveller in the rain forest. The climate of this partial zone is affected by the monsoon, hence the dry season. Botanists are drawn here because they can see special ecologic phenomena including buttress roots, which really are quite a sight, sometimes sprouting from the tree trunk thirty feet up, but those of a nervous disposition should steer well clear of the Awful Hanging Experts.

## Brace Yerself, Morag

Beavers are being reintroduced to Scotland, we understand, so there may be opportunities for international expansion for this Canadian firm.

## No Teasing

It means 'Do not disturb the animals' but the slight mistranslation is better.

## No Touching

Parents out shopping with their children are forever telling them not to touch the goods but in China, the land of well behaved children, tourist adults get their own special warning.

请勿戏弄动物

Please don't hurt the animals
while teasing them

# Please don't touch yourself , Let us help you to try out. Thanks !

# A WOMAN'S WORK IS NEVER DONE

Who does the ironing in former Soviet republics, and why does a Chinese manufacturer choose English as his passport to megasales?

Here we are in Kazakhstan, where the sun always shines and 'er indoors dashes away with the smoothing iron, smiling in a bikini, ironing in a garden full of palm trees, blissfully unaware of the smell of scorching polyester.

It's a well-known fact that the Chinese are very fond of crosswords – at least, they like the cryptic intricacies of the clues. They do have crossword puzzles in Chinese but the nature of Chinese characters make them devilishly awkward, so the Chinese produce crosswords in English, with predictable results.

This enthusiasm has clearly caught on at the advertising agency, and anyone solving the clue, 'Red valuably enters wan home', gets a free Burns The Clothes Board. The Four Big Merits of the Burns The Clothes Board are most attractive to prospective purchasers, being:

(a) **Artistic Reliable Is Practical,**

(b) **The All Steelfoot Rest Spurts Models,**

(c) **Four Altitude Mixture Controls, and**

(d) **Entire Cotton and Kapow Cotton Print.**

# LIBERATE YOUR BODY

...with the help of four mechanical engineers. Live on a blue planet.

**Jinhua Fit Industry & Development Co., Ltd devotes to R&D these products that can assist you in enjoying all of the chosen sports for maximum pleasure. Our product line includes kayak trolley, canoe trolley, Stand Up Paddle Board and Windsurfer Trolleys and even outdoor gears. Our goal is to liberate your body and make you enjoy the sporting item heart and soul.**

**Our products are directly designed by Industry Leaders that have been involved around the Water sports and Golfing Fields for more than 25 years. Our Industry & Development Co has four skilled mechanical engineers who have been engaged in mechanical R&D**

**for more than a decade. We pay more attention to every detail of our products. We vow to offer you our excellent services. Our vision is to keep providing high quality products and services by which we can gain our customers' trust and establish our sound reputation. We will make all of our efforts to offer our best-in-class selections and work closely with our clients in defining their needs. Hereby, Jinhua Fit Industry & Development Co. is the name you can trust. Live on a blue planet and enjoy.**

As we are unable, for one reason or another, to bring you a picture of a best-in-class selection or, indeed,

of anything even slightly relevant to the Jinhua Fit Industry and Development Co, instead we show you fitness as illustrated by this early experiment in break-dancing.

## PULL THE OTHER ONE

You can count on the fingers of two hands the number of towns in the world that have made fortunes out of the objects marked 'pull' on the ends of lavatory chains. There are those towns that correspond to Arnold Bennett's famous five – Stoke, Burslem, Tunstall, Hanley, Longton – plus the one he forgot, Fenton, plus Komaki, a pleasant if otherwise unremarkable town north of Nagoya on Honshu.

Home-made examples of lavvy pulls, such as the one pictured, which used to be the handle of a hacksaw, were commonplace when the high-level cistern was the flush method of choice. Sometimes, people didn't even bother with that

The home-made option was often the resort of poorer households, but fashionable society always preferred the real thing.

and just had a knot on the end of a piece of string. Very likely, they also had the *Daily Express* torn into squares, stuck on a nearby nail.

In those glorious days, when Bronco and San Izal ruled and nobody had ever heard of Andrex, the most fashionable lavvy pull thing was the Honen Matsuri brand, sold by the thousand in hardware shops everywhere.

When the modern low-level cistern came into style, with its simple metal or plastic handle (see pictures), the potteries of Staffordshire found it easy enough to switch to other products such as Royal Doulton tea services. In Japan, WC development was

Here we have more examples of how progress is not always for the better. Surely pressing a rinky-dink little handle cannot equal the satisfaction to be had from a good strong pull with resultant powerful flush.

slower and so Honen Matsuri brand could dominate the domestic and regional markets for many more years. Today, all of the families in Komaki continue to owe their existence in some way to the several factories' successful designs.

Despite the reduction of the high-level cistern to the status of architectural salvage, the debt to the symbol of Komaki's prosperity is still celebrated every year, on March 1, when selected virgins and other youthful persons parade holding giant replicas.

One enormous example is wheeled through the streets as it were in a funeral procession, by workers who lost their jobs when the factories closed.

Visitors to the fête from other areas can buy souvenirs in plaster of Paris, on sale in the shops, including battery-powered models that move to replicate the original pulling action. You can also get a kind of Groucho Marx disguise with a Honen Matsuri theme, which may come in handy for fancy-dress parties.

Incidentally, 'nazi' is Swahili for coconut.

# YOU'LL WONDER WHERE THE YELLOW WENT

The MD of Hawley & Hazel Chemical Co, then based in Shanghai, went on a visit to the US in the early 1930s and saw Al Jolson on stage. The singer, in top hat and tails and black make-up, with a dazzling smile, looked like a brilliant idea for a toothpaste brand. Darkie was born and very successful it became.

After Colgate purchased fifty percent of the firm in 1985, all manner of folk protested at the racially offensive nature of the brand, but the company didn't want to change it because it made so much money.

Three years and more later, Colgate switched the name from Darkie to Darlie, with a TV ad showing a cartoon character carrying a letter L to change with the K. They modified the logo to a Frankie Vaughan version, and paid for all the relaunch advertising and the new packaging.

While it now says Darlie in English, in Chinese it says the same as it did before – black man, black people or African toothpaste – and at the time of writing, still does. As the Colgate statement put it: 'The morally right thing dictated that we must change (in a way) that is least damaging to the economic interests of our partners.'

**Hawley & Hazel's toothpaste products, sold under the Darlie brand, are a bestselling household name throughout the region. Today, Darlie toothpaste is one of the market leaders in China, Hong Kong, Taiwan, Singapore, Malaysia and Thailand, synonymous with clean white teeth and a confident smile everywhere.**

Or, as they sing in the morning on the way to work in Malaysia, *Gigi sihat, senyum memikat* (Alluring smile teeth).

# ORAL OFFENCE AND THE TOOTH FAIRY

Someone should tell her

(BUT NOBODY DOES)

Many a girl never finds out why her romances fizzle out. That's because, much as they dislike Oral Offence, people just can't bring themselves to tell a girl she's guilty of it. Scientific tests prove that in 7 cases out of 10 Colgate Dental Cream stops Oral Offence that originates in the mouth.

1/3 Inc. Tax.

PLAY SAFE!
USE

COLGATE
RIBBON DENTAL CREAM

TWICE
A DAY

**Many a girl never finds out why her romances fizzle out. That's because, much as they dislike Oral Offence, people just can't bring themselves to tell a girl she's guilty of it.**

Colgate's narrative soft sell of 1947, promising to stop Oral Offence that originates in the mouth, will not do for modern times. White Jade toothpaste, type 89, is made in China:

**You will keep fresh after use. Your teeth will be health and no usual oral disease can occur. White Jade for smokers (super cleaning) toothpaste is new product. It does no harm to animal, it for smokers quite well.**

Not aimed at Chinese smoking animals, you can also get West Man toothpaste, which has a picture of a cowboy on the pack, and Cool Mate, which contains gargle elements. Which brings us to Clogard, a successful Sri Lankan toothpaste:

> ...adopting a more endearing platform for its brand communications. Despite being a relatively young brand, Clogard is perceived as being steeped in local heritage. This is a result of its close correlation with clove oil. The first commercial on this new platform used three generations and the close-to-the-heart idiom of the squirrel – the local equivalent of the tooth fairy. The commercial made it to Nielsen's list of top recalled advertising in Sri Lanka. The most recent extension of this campaign continues to use three generations – grandmother, mother and grandson – and another local idiom of losing milk teeth to an elephant and relying on Clogard to ensure the health of permanent teeth.

So now you know.

Did you MACLEAN your teeth today?

A brilliant exhibition

MACLEANS Peroxide Tooth Paste makes teeth WHITER

## THE GIRL WITH THE VERY LARGE MUFF

As we can see from the pictures, the fashion in muffs tended towards larger and larger examples until, as is so often the way of things, the item itself fell entirely from favour. There was a short period when a skimpy, skinny kind of a muff was fashionable but so lacking in function that really it was only suitable for the summer, which rather defeats the object.

Flourishing briefly after being spotted among the nymphs of Rio de Janeiro, the minimalist muff made way for an even more Spartan look. Indeed, nowadays, if a lady is to present herself as a style totem, she must do without a muff altogether.

Be that as it may, in the more backward capitals of Europe, in this case Talinn, where winters can be harsh, there remains a market for hand-me-downs.

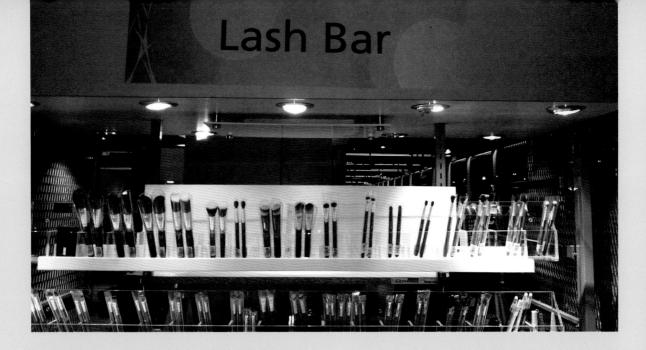

Lash Bar

## *What Are They Flogging?*

Why are they selling artists' materials in the Lash Bar, Kuala Lumpur? Is this a front for a dodgy S&M establishment? No, they're only make-up brushes for your eye lashes.

## CPR Free

Perhaps it's the prices. Perhaps they're selling Korean Coolpis jeans in this shop in Kuala Lumpur, Malaysia. Coolpis is also a Korean soft drink, one flavour of which is kim chee, the explosive type of saueskraut they make with vast quantities of garlic and chilli.

## ALL IN THE MIND

The double entendre can be part of the Law of Unintended Consequences, which states that any action to change anything, whether or not it has the intended consequence, will have at least one that was unintended.

So, when the boys at Bushmills distillery decided to call their special blend Black Bush, they had no idea that, one day, a man whose special preference was for Irish whiskey would go into a pub with which he was unfamiliar, where the barmaid was an olive-skinned, Spanish-looking beauty with long, very dark hair. This man, equally unaware of the aforementioned law, said 'Do you have a large Black Bush?'

Possibly the ad-agency copywriter on the Sanatogen account was a lady inexperienced in male physiology, or perhaps someone somewhere was taking the Mick, or maybe they were prepared to ignore the smirks and chortles of the mucky-minded

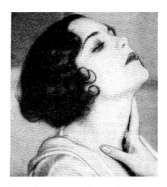

Chesterfield. Blow some my way.

Lucky Strike. So round, so firm, so fully packed.

It takes two hands to hold a Whopper.

majority, but 'Sanatogen prevents morning stiffness' ran as a headline for quite a while in the 1970s.

When the Americans decided to use a woman in a cigarette ad for the first time, in 1926, they had her sitting on a rock by the sea, as you can see. Her handsome companion was lighting up, and she was saying 'Blow some my way'. The copy below said that nothing could equal natural tobacco taste; get that, and you get everything.

This seems a little too direct in linking sex with drugs and rock and roll, so we hesitantly offer our own ideas of how that ad and a couple of others might have been improved in their subtlety. We have had to save money by using the same model for all three, but you get the idea.

# THE LAZU FOD

Some years ago, the brilliant humorist Paul Jennings wrote about 'Psychotyping' for one of his *Observer* columns, in which he expressed his amazement that anyone could type without looking at the keys. When he tried it, he discovered a hidden talent as a typewriter medium, turning ordinary words and phrases into a kind of surreal poetry, defying interpretation by normal methods. Thus the standard typing line containing all the letters of the alphabet became:

> *the quicj brown hox ji ji jumoef over the lazu fod*
> *or*
> *The quick briwn fox jiumoec the quock bobrow*

Echos of Edward Lear and 'The Jabberwocky' can clearly be seen, but the problem for the rest of us, who do not have Jennings's psycho-gift or Lear's genius, or a typewriter, is how to generate such poetry of our own.

The answer could lie in collecting comical Malayan and Chinese signs as a kind of art trouvé and recomposing them into lines with rhythm and hidden meaning.

Please do not see it
While drinking the drink.
Please see the thing which
The chief does not have.
Thangs you for come,
The pet bottle caps it.
Thangs you for come,
While drinking the drink
To fisiting us
And put in a bag.

> **Please do not see it while drinking drink.**
>
> The PET bottle caps it and put it in a bag and please carry it.
> Please see the thing which the chief does not have after finishing drinking.

Another possibility is internet translation tools. Here is part of a German eBay ad for a guitar, translated into English by Google:

Of course she has a few scratches,
But that also is no shame.
This is a top instrument is dated
Sounded forth all brands other large equal birth.
Privatverfauf, no warranty or jerk opinion.

This is blank verse, admittedly, but still challenging enough for any stream-of-consciousness poet to have composed unaided, even if one recognises that Privatverfauf is a typing error for Privatverkauf, private sale, which - of course - no googly thingery would spot.

'Mary had a little lamb' translated into Hungarian by an automatic translation service comes out as Mary volt barikám which, translated back into English becomes 'It was Mary barikam'. Using an online dictionary, we find that barika is Hungarian for baal-lamb, which is a bit spooky.

A mysterious legend on a Spanish toothpaste called Genial, made in China, reveals another poet, hidden in Google or maybe in a Chinese toothpaste factory:

**Los finos Micro Granulos de la crema dental Floppi Restriegon suavemente la superficie de los dientes y en media de ellos**

...which translates as:

**The fine microgranules**
**Of toothpaste Floppi Restriegon**
**Gently from the teeth surface**
**And half of them.**

Cycles Sirius

14 & 16, Rue Duret, PARIS

## BABY, YOU CAN DRIVE MY CAR

There's something of a branding folktale about the Vauxhall Nova. In Spanish, you could say *No va* is 'doesn't go', but only if in English you would construe 'novice' as demanding saintly behaviour. In Portuguese, nova means the news.

Pajero, as in Mitsubishi car, does mean wanker in Spanish, and the Buick LaCrosse can mean something very similar in Canadian French. The Nissan Cedric, now a cult vehicle in Australia, was so named because the big boss of Nissan took to a character of that name in *Little Lord Fauntleroy* and thought it would go down well with westerners wanting a luxury car. It's successor, the Fuga, means flight or hurry in some of the Romance languages, which is good, but it means grout in Polish.

The Mazda LaPuta is the prostitute in Spanish and Portuguese, and the word puta is used with other short words to make some very foul language indeed. Honda Fitta became the Jazz when somebody realised that *fitta*, in impolite parts of Sweden and Norway, is a vulgar term for a lady's front bottom.

Polo, the mint with the hole, becomes a different kind of hole when it's a Polo GT in Spanish, and the super go-faster Toyota MR2 in French is the *em-air-deux*, which is almost merde and could be Toyota *est merde* in a song. In India, Hindi speakers giggle at the Skoda Laura and at any other poor Laura, for she is a penis to them.

We could go on, and on. In the good old days, when semi-naked girls rode bicycles side-saddle through the streets of Paris and cars had names like T, and 8, there was no need to worry. We buy any car was the general opinion, if we could afford it and were prepared to put the work in to keep it going.

Then, we had the time when cars had names like Sovereign, Super Snipe and Prefect, Herald, Zodiac and Ital, which surely were not open to misinterpretation, although Rolls Royce are said to have been careful to employ Silver Cloud rather than Silver Mist, as mist is ordure in German.

Anyway, the marketing chaps started getting worried, so names became deliberately meaningless except, despite all their efforts, they always do mean something in some language or other.

So, the only safe thing to do is go back. Let's hear it for the Vauxhall 6 and the Ford Scarborough.

Minx doesn't seem to mean anything in any major language, although the Italian word for flirty flibbertigibbet is civetta, and autocivetta is an unmarked police car.

# DON'T BUILD YOUR BRAND ON SHIFTING SAND

Back in the USA in 1925, motor cars were not plentiful outside the cities and country roads were rubbish, so the idea of promoting a shaving soap with roadside signs seemed too outrageous for Clinton Odell, inventor of Burma-Shave brushless shaving cream. His sons Alan and Leonard persuaded him otherwise, and soon there were thousands of them all across America. The little signs came in series of five or six, spelling out a verse as you drove along:

> **Shaving brushes**
> **You'll soon see 'em**
> **On a shelf**
> **In some museum.**
> **Burma-Shave.**

There were many favourites:

> **My job is keeping faces clean, and nobody knows de stubble I've seen.**
> **This cream makes the gardener's daughter, plant her tu-lips where she oughter.**

One that caused a sensation was:

> **It's free, it's free, a trip to Mars, for 900 empty jars.**

Mad jar collectors were eventually told it was a one-way trip. Lots featured road safety messages, but the original and typical angle was more commercial:

**Use our shave,**
**and we betcha,**
**the girls won't wait,**
**they'll come and getcha.**

The last signs went up in 1963, the campaign and the product having been overtaken by aspects of civilisation undreamed of in 1925 – freeways, millions and millions of motor cars travelling faster and faster, vast roadside hoardings, and electric shavers.

One nostalgic fan put his own signs up:

**Farewell, O verse, along the road.**
**How sad to see you're out of mode.**

The cream itself is no longer made but the brand lives on, would you believe, on the Burma Shave Shaving Brush.

# BARREL SCRAPING DEPARTMENT

According to a survey, Kenco is the 104th superbrand, out of the 500 brand names most recognised by UK citizens. Nescafé is 44th and Douwe Egberts 68th. Mind you, some of the results make you wonder who was in the research sample, when Playstation, Nintendo, Hornby and Scalextric are all in the first hundred, while The Co-op, Radio Times, Argos and Flora are in the 350s and Tampax, Mr Sheen and Wonderbra are in the 360s.

Any road up, as a superbrand just outside the top 100, it is clearly a priority for the Kenco marketing department to increase the pressure and try to bear down on those other coffees, hence the brilliant ploy of using a jar with 7% less glass* (*Compared to previous jar). We look forward to the superbrand tables next year to see the improvement this has brought about.

They're even more desperate at Breville, not in the 500 at all. The message with a new Breville kettle read 'Don't just boil it. Breville it!'.

Smeg, by the way, was placed at number 171.

# BRAND NEW LOOK!

# 7% LESS GLASS*

*Compared to previous jar

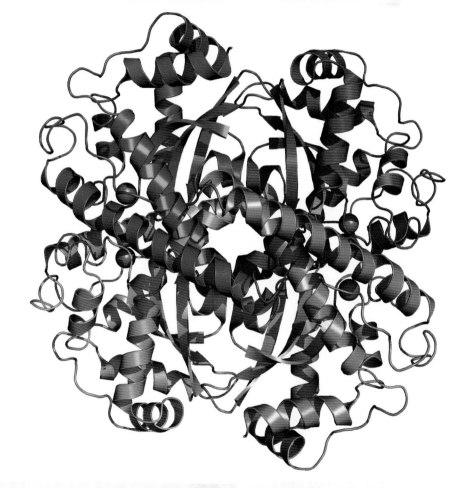

# HANG ON, SLOOPY.

**Marrow, a spongy tissue, exists in meshes among the marrow cavity of long bones and sloopy sclerotin of flat bones.**

Sclerotin is an organic stiffening component of, for example, the biting mouthparts of scorpions. What makes it sloopy, we don't know. Possibly Chairman Liang Jun Zhang of the beautiful and harmonious Green World Group may know. He, after all, sojourned the Republic of Ghana and had amiable deliberation there, and has discussed herb planting with Mr Goodwill Zwelithini, King of Zulu. But please, read on.

**Compound Marrow Powder is a nutritious health food. It takes fresh spinal cord, brain marrow, cavity marrow of cow, lecithin, protein powder, buckwheat powder, multivitamin, and trace elements such as Fe, Zinc, Mg, as its ingredients, thus supplement the body with various nutrient. Compound Marrow Powder can increase human immunity, relieve fatigue, improve sleepiness, enhance memory, regulate blood lipid, balance blood pressure, retard aging, alleviate sore of waist and pain of leg, supplement body with calcium, help osteoporosis, increase SOD activity and calcium level in blood serum.**

SOD activity? This has become very fashionable in circles where the word 'antioxidant' is bandied about. The diagram is not, as might be thought, the design for an Olympic Games logo nor even for an olympic stadium, but rather an explanation - if one were needed - of the structure of a typical superoxide dismutase, or SOD.

# iSHINE BENEFITS WIT

Along with your cavity marrow of cow, you should also be taking the Green World iShine Capsule. This is nothing to do with iPods. It's a capsule, made by the company that promises to empower and enable you to have the tool by which you can materialise your desire to enjoy a personal financial freedom. It's a kind of sleeping pill.

**Long term insomnia and bad sleep may decline the immune function and quicken aging, etc. Green World iShine Capsule is extracted and processed from natural plants.**

**Polygala Tenuifolia calms the nerves, hastens sleep, lessens dream, soothes the nerves and benefits wit.**

**Herba Gynostemmae Pentaphylli contains mercaptan and more than 50 kinds of saponins, which brings quiet sleep and placid mood, improves mental involvement, enhances brain function and boosts memory.**

**Radix Curcumae dissipates stasis of qi, alleviates mental depression, and enhances sleep quality.**

**The combination works wonderfully. It regulates sleep, brings the sleep from the shallower to the deeper and then to the sleeping state quickly.**

**iShine Capsule has an obvious effect on climacteric insomnia, unknown cause insomnia, fidget, anxiety, hypomnesis, dizzy, tinnitus and fatigue caused by insomnia, dream disturbed sleep, and waking up with a start at night.**

**iShine Capsule harmonizes the balance between excitement and restrain of pallium cells. Suggested Use: 10-15 minutes before sleep.**

Botanical note: Polygala tenuifolia, also known as Chinese senega, Yuan Zhi, offers a root extract used in traditional Chinese medicine to reduce senior moments. The leaves of Gynostemma pentaphyllum, a kind of gourd, make Jiaogulan, the Tea of Immortality, while the root of Curcuma longa, turmeric, makes a powder that turns everything bright yellow. Qi (or chi) means breath but in this context represents the life force.

Always take your iShine ten to fifteen minutes before sleep. You may need assistance if you wish to take it later, but at least you won't wake up with a start.

BODY SELEB 灼熱系ボディメイク
Red Heat Hot pepper

# SHAPE UP GEL

シェイプアップジェル グレープフルーツの香り

I can't join the party due to
ugly body. I am now in
shape-up mode. Some day
I will do it with dress up.
BODY SELEB is willing to help you to achieve
it. The success gives you self-confidence. Let's go
to the party where a lot of celeb gather. You will
see yourself changed drastically.

# *MAD ABOUT THE BOYS No 1*

While Healthy Boy would surely have won the bonniest baby competition at the village fete in 1955, he is maybe a little portly for the modern view.

'With strong intention to maintain the quality, Healthy Boy products are publicly accepted among, in particular, Thai dishes and Chinese dishes,' says visionary chairman Mr Vichien Tangsombatvisit of the Yan Wal Yun Co.

The company's production facility in Samutsakorn was hailed as a great prize to our chairman, as reflected in his well-known statement:

> **We have been and will remain committed to continuous development, to offer quality products and services to our valued customers.**

Not quite so well known is the Thai for healthy boy, which is deksomboon. Yan Wal Yun Co also offers something else that has nothing to do with iPads or iMacs, viz, the not very well known i-Chef brand of cook-in-sauce mixes.

The Sweet Chilli Sauce is most appetizing for fried, grilled or special menu dishes such as Hot, Sweet and Sour Grouper. The same firm makes Maxchup tomato ketchup with no oriental taste.

## MAD ABOUT THE BOYS No 2

Billy Boy is Germany's excitingly different condom, rigorously tested to meet German quality standards. Be young, have fun, and don't settle for anything less.

We may think the makers have missed an opportunity, perhaps not understanding the potential of that other abbreviation of William, but they have a long tradition of marketing in a jolly way, with none of the under-the-counter embarrassment that characterised the old British approach to the barber or the Boots Saturday girl. For example, there is an energy drink, with a picture on the tin of Billy Boy juggling with fruit, and he appears elsewhere as Super Billy Boy with a big B on his, er, chest.

Quite why he has taken up ice hockey on a German cigarette lighter, with a legend that translates as Some Like it Harder, we can only speculate. The lighters, incidentally, were manufactured under licence by Curly and Smooth GmbH, which also makes sunglasses with flags on them:

**the ideal taking along article for coming sports events. If soccer, motorsports or any other event with these sunglasses you can show your nationality! Never use them if you depent on activities where you need your eyesight.**

Billy Boy eagerly awaits his chance to meet the German brand of potato dumplings, Pfanni.

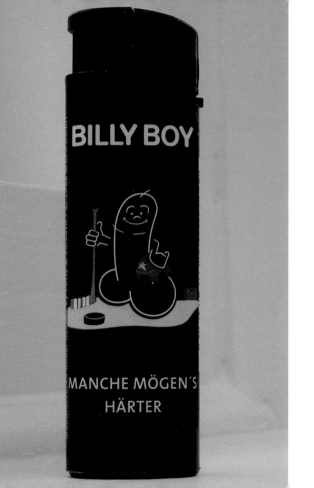

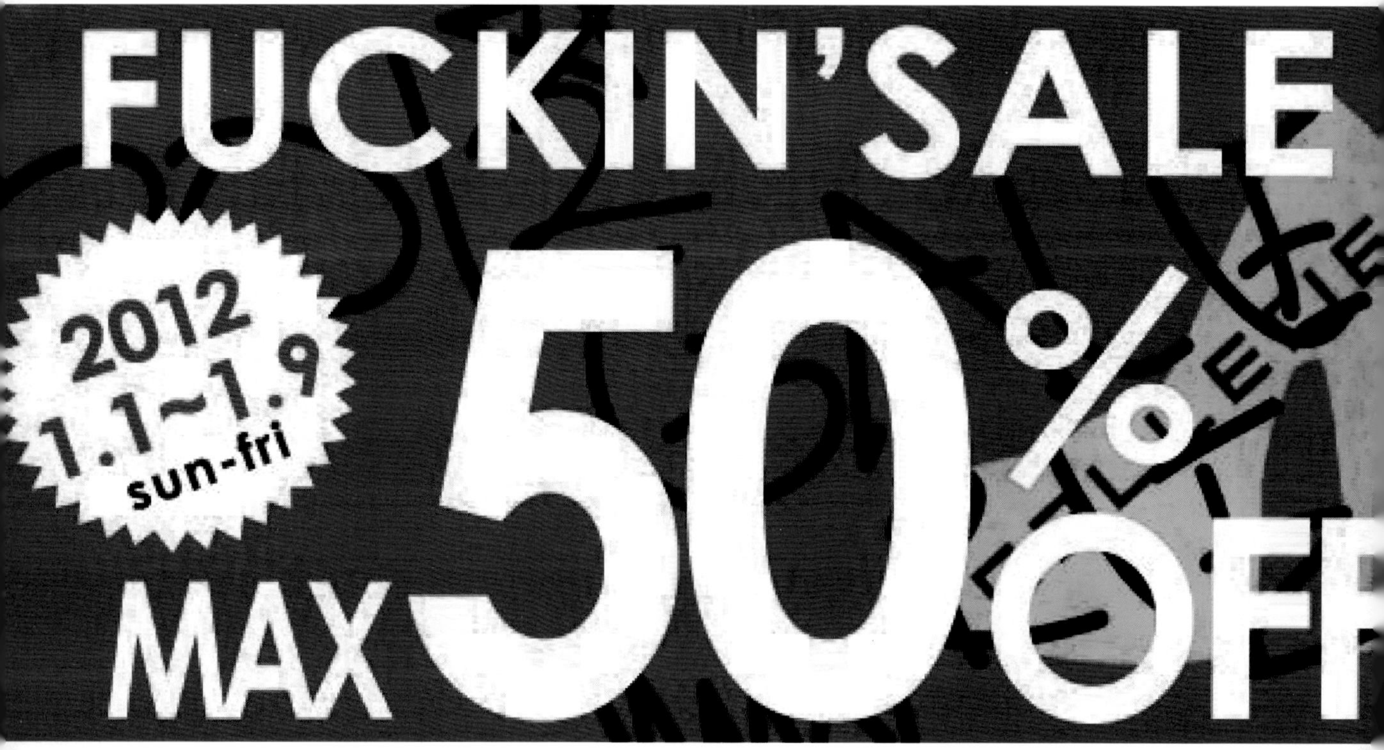
FUCKIN'SALE
2012
1.1~1.9
sun-fri
MAX 50%OFF

## Indecent Discounts!

Twenty per cent off what, we want to know? As this appears to be a clothes shop rather than a house of ill repute, we have to assume that the discount is on garments and the wording is an expression of enthusiasm.

## The Abba Snack

Knowing me, knowing you – AHA! It's a Polish sesame-seed toffee crisp.

## CARRY ON CAMPING

What can we say about this shop in Salzburg? Is there anything we can possibly add? No, is the answer.

# WON'T YOU CHOO-CHOO ME HOME?

It is not uncommon among gentlefolk of a certain age to feel left behind by the new technology. Just how far had not been apparent to your correspondent, until he happened upon this entirely novel application for a portable telephone.

**Ring-a-Buzz vibrates not only to the signal of your mobile phone, but also works manually. Simply slide it into your erogeneous zone and let yourself go. Use the big round button to adjust the ultimate vibration you want or wait for a call or text to experience an erotic vibration.**

Wait for a text? From whom? The person sitting opposite on the train? Is that why people ignore the signs in the quiet carriage?

Readers are invited to spot the Ring-a-Buzz user in this Pullman railway carriage.

# ATTRACTIVE TO HIS MEAT

How do you make Vietnamese spring rolls, or Banh trang phoi suong? It happens behind the gates (pictured) of Dien Khanh, in Khanh Hoa province. It is quite a complicated process and so we thought we'd better have the recipe in full. By all means try this at home, but only on dewy mornings.

**According to the baker since then to make the fog roll drying, material goods are delicious and the rice is not mixed. If the roll elsewhere or add sugar to soften the bread, then roll an additional pinch of salt fog exposure, so when birds eat the cake, you will feel the salt cake. After powder coated two-layer cake (the cake so thick), then dried in the sun offers. Two new phases formed after the cake, the cake was designed a special oven, which is burned material shell peanuts. Rice paper drying is complete peanuts cooked over the fire, I can not just grilled over inflated to nine.**

**Then the wheels are classified separately, waiting to sleep early morning when dew began to fall more (check by looking at the trees), new offer roll out dry fog, the scientists also exposed to mist the sun wheel to consciousness with wheels, fog proof enough just waiting for bread is soft folded immediately, put in the bag, lined with banana leaves. When selling a put out a new course, always wrapped in a plastic bag to giucho soft bread always. Rice paper drying mist, like rice paper rolls rice paper production in marine village, Dien Khanh, Khanh Hoa is embedded khongcan water when being used.**

The dry fog roll only attractive to his meat. Many people joked that nothing more sophisticated presentation drawings, but just to Trang Bang, try eating a meat roll rolling fog exposure, understand how the dish of pork roll rolling boil again become a real name.

I looked at the plate brought vegetables, see the fancy of the dish. Many vegetables are very strange. Even the few who work in the shop, reading the names of obvious cheap vegetables. Rau contributed to the honor roll. I only told a few vegetables for nearly 20 kinds of vegetables on the table, but there are many kinds of vegetables by owner sometimes have to reserve in advance, have only the forest type or land of Trang Bang. Rau to be exposed to frost his cake coated pork must be 5 Taste: acrid, sweet, sour, fatty, aromatic. It's lettuce, shiso, chives leaves, leaf frogs, leaf crest chancre, talisman, Melaleuca guava leaf, basil, basil slip, need water, the moon, chancroid and chestnut leaves, the cinnamon, coriander ship, then there is more long-chopped cucumber, pickles and sprouts. The leaves warts, chancroid chestnut, indigo guava leaf meal at the new South. And the sauce is very simple look, it's just delicious sauce is made. But mixing sauces are also catching breath. Particularly to eat pork roll is exposed to frost ham, the meat of the pig. Raw meat is cooked, place the chopped white and very tasty and soft.

A pork roll book full of vegetables that, put sauce, eat enough to feel the taste of grass. In vegetable salads, cakes wrapped contribute.

# I'M IN PIECES, BITS AND PIECES

Everybody has sore bits from time to time. Your correspondent, his bits made sore by walking on wet mountains, once rubbed Fiery Jack on them by mistake. Sorbits is a popular name in Denmark, used in veterinary products as well as sugar-free chews for oral hygiene. There is, or was, a Danish-bred cairn terrier called Mr Winterbottom's Sorbits.

A tit can be a small horse, a small bird (titmouse), a hussy, a slap as in tit for tat, or a vulgar shortening of teat. Tid is a dialect word meaning tender and sweet, hence tid-bit, whence tit-bit. Here it is little packets of aromatic seeds and whatnot to freshen your breath after a curry, called in Hindi

mukhwas. Tit-Bit Foods of Mumbai is a big operator in mukhwas and other products that outshine the rest in their quality and are in demand by discerning users in the four corners of the world, for example:

**Convenience foods have become the order of the day, mainly due to the upsurge of nuclear families, and more working women. On the other hand, Continental and Oriental cooking enjoy more popularity than ever before. Tit-Bit recognizes these two trends and is the first to capitalize on them by introducing a product range that has never been attempted before - instant Chinese Gravy Mixes - that let you prepare authentic Chinese in a jiffy.**

One definition of a jiffy is $3 \times 10^{-44}$ seconds, which is really not very much time at all.

# GESUNDHEIT

As they say at Mucos HQ in Berlin, somewhat enigmatically, prevention and maintaining proper health is becoming more relevant than the treatment of disease itself.

The German health product called Mucos offers **Gesund mit Enzymen. Taking enzymes can assist the body own enzymes. One great advantage to enzyme treatment is that it is nearly side effect free. This preventive method strengthens the patient's overall immune system, without adding burdening symptoms.**

Being nearly side effect free, we can only assume that any symptoms added by taking Mucos are of the non-burdening variety.

# THINGS GO BETTER WITH LOVE BODY

Squirt is a grapefruity soda pop which has been refreshing thirsty Americans since 1938, when a chap called Herb Bishop formulated it in Phoenix, Arizona, or maybe it was another chap called Peter Hodde in Detroit, Michigan. Anyway, it's an ingredient in such famous cocktails as Mike's Pimp Juice, and is owned by Dr Pepper.

Love Body, owned by Coca Cola, is made with tea and is sold as a dietary aid in Japan. Other dietary aids available there include Diet Water and Water Salad, the latter perhaps being marginally more fattening than just the water, although maybe not as it is supposed to take more energy to digest lettuce than you get from it.

## Nuts Downunder

Nobby's is really a blokey Australian brand, made in UK by Walker's Crisps, which is Pepsico, although it doesn't say so on the packet. For more on nobs, see page 20. The 1970s chain of Knobs and Knockers shops seems to have disappeared although there are various outfits similarly named. Quite what that has to do with the price of fish, we cannot say.

## Size Matters

Look, the way to sell these little bags of peanuts at a premium price is to name them after a bra size. We put a Page 3 girl on the card, who may or may not be a D cup, nobody's going to worry, we put the card in the pub and, as the bags are pulled off, all is revealed, or nearly all. The poor girl has a big hole in her face for the nail, but who cares? Forty years later, still going. Brilliant, or what?

# CRUMBS

The Japanese breadcrumb method was invented and developed in Japan. We started breadcrumb manufacture in 1967 and built up the workforce from 5 to 650, following the dietary changes in Japan in the 70s. We are very proud of our key role in enriching the dietary life of the Japanese people, and to a lesser extent people overseas, through the production of breadcrumbs Our electrically and oven breadcrumbs are soft and hard, yellow, white and orange, and certified Halal. As a company, we play an important role socially, and will continue in our efforts to make people's dietary life more enjoyable.

# DICK ME NO DICKS

'Dick me no Dicks' is a remark fictionally attributed to Nell Gwynn by Irish writer Frank Frankfort Moore, although what she meant by it we have no idea. It could equally well have been said in a meeting of Heinz's marketing department, brackets, puddings, for the old tin that had SPOTTED DICK emblazoned in cocksure fashion has been coyly dumbed down.

Now, as you can see, it's a taste of home delightful pudding, in case you thought it was a riding whip or a leather apron.

Big Dick's Halfway Inn, Home of the Minnow Shot, is by a lake in Missouri. They keep a tank of live minnows in the bar. You select one to go in your tot of vodka, whisky or whatever and, toasting Burl Ives (who knew an old lady who swallowed a fly), down it goes, wriggle wriggle. For those insufficiently confident to face

Big Dick's, there is also a Skinny Dick's Halfway Inn way up north in Alaska.

Mini Dickmann's might look like suppositories but they are very nice. The firm that makes them has kept up the connection by acquiring the bittermints of Messrs Bendick.

NOW EVEN MORE GINGERY!

## *McNutty*

Americans find McVitie's Ginger Nuts one of the world's most amusing biscuits. In Britain, home to ever more gingery nuts, we dip them in our tea without a second thought.

### McTarty

Flaky these puffs may be, but there is no German
language copy on the packet for a quite different
reason. Puff in German is brothel.

# FRIED ICE CREAM AND YEE SANG TOSSING

Next time you're in Penang, or anywhere in Malaysia, you will surely be unable to resist buying The Beautiful Food, the 'essential drip of the bees with a gorgeous taste to quench your beautiful day.'

Should you fancy some yee sang for lunch, it may well have been prepared off the premises by Spring Toss Food Service, or you can have a take-away.

**This prepacked Yee Sang with gold bullion packaging packed with good blessing elements, hope to bring prosperity to anyone who have joined the yee sang tossing fiesta.**

Yee sang, of course, is a kind of fish carpaccio with dipping sauces and salads (see picture), associated especially with the Chinese new year which is celebrated in many countries outside China, including Malaysia. One ingredient in the salad can be banana flowers (pictured in dried form overleaf) which, when soaked, taste vaguely of figs and are otherwise known as vazhai poo.

Blaze Local Snacks will take the bite right out of you. Blaze has found from observation that mostly Europeans and people from the Americas have a strong affection for their snacks. They go very well with alcoholic beverages.

**Valued customers who have preference for hot and spicy food may like Sincerity Meatball, with a very chewable outer layer and encrusted with hot aromatic meat and soup. It's fun but be cautious if you serve it hot.**

Aiskrim Goreng? We've heard of Nasi Goreng, so if Aiskrim is what we think it might be, we indeed have Fried Ice Cream. Yes. . .

> **our special products is Fit 3 Fried Ice Cream. Its is made using bread and ice cream selected. After frying, our produk will be crispy, crunchy and not oily, suitable with our tagline "Satisfaction with each bite".**

Homemade Chocolates might be better.

> **The Ultimate Favourite Food for all Chocoholics beware;**
> **Will likely make you drool all over the pages.**

Further exploration of the Malaysian peninsula can reveal Smart Diko chocolate drink, Kampung Kerisik coconut paste, Pet Double Camel Sauce Light King which, disappointingly, is only a brand of soy sauce, Four Season Beverage Stuff, Horse Milk Candy (yes, sweeties made out of mare's milk, and why not), Deep Blue Sheep Placenta capsules, Jacker Wafer Cube, Six Star Mucle, the mysterious Usplabs, Rainbow Cock Gummy Candy and, to freshen up after the feast, Brutal Lotion for Men.

Dadih Powder is not, as fevered imaginations might want to believe, an aphrodisiac but rather a kind of Malaysian Angel Delight.

## Chocolate Greens

In America, they have 'taken the yuk out of eating vegetables'. Amazing Grass Kidz Superfood combines 33 fruits and vegetables in a delicious chocolate drink powder. Just one serving of this 70% organic drink with outrageous chocolate flavor equals three of your five a day. You can get the other two by eating pizza, which has been classified as a vegetable in the US so that pizza manufacturers' products can continue to feature in subsidised school meals, which must include a goodly amount of, er, vegetables.

## Now Wash Your Hands

Stripwinkel is Dutch for comic shop, and Dumpie is a downwardly mobile under-employed middle-aged professional, who may well be the type of person to patronise comic-book shops, or a Scottish kind of hen, or possibly a cartoon canine. This one is in Leiden, a really lovely town in the best Dutch canal/cafe tradition.

## Stung Again

These very fine premises on Zelny street in Brno, Czech Republic, belong to realitní kancelá_ Sting, which is to say, estate agent.

## COOLDOG KABOOM

Older readers will remember Passing Clouds, WD & HO Wills's version of the Turkish cigarette, oval rather than round and much more aromatic than plain Virginia. Readers even older than that may remember Eran-Khayyam, here offering a free bottle of perfume with every shilling box of fags tipped with a rose petal, silk or gold, and all of the rarest vintage that could grace the banquet of thoughts. They are normally only available in the harems of Constantinople or the palaces of India's Native Princes, and they might as well be for all the tobacconists there are left on the high street. A guinea an ounce, for younger readers, would translate as about €225 for 25 grams.

In modern Turkey they still smoke a lot but also offer Cooldog complete dog food, Islek frozen laying hens, Bekap frozen chicken paws with luggage labels so they won't get lost and, for confused Cinderellas, Golden Glass Pumpkin. It is excessively ambitious product!!!.

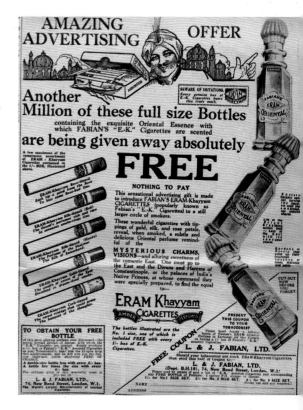

The Ornek company produces small and big elbows with line or without line (no mystery - it's pasta), with which you might like some salami or bologna mince from the Doga Food Company.

You might think about a silk-tipped ciggie for afterwards if you have Kaboom Sexual Food, Tuskon instant drink powder, or Sexual Drink from Dad Food Service of Ankara.

> **Both men and women can use before sex. Coffee effects will begin after using 1 hour and continues 48 hours. Can use with alcohol.**

If that doesn't work, try Romeo Juliet capsules.

> **Feel the effects within 20 minutes. Experience a harder and longer lasting erection (4 days).**

The magic medicine concocted in the sixteenth century for the mother of Suleyman the Magnificent, known as Mesir, is thrown annually from the top of the Sultan Mosque in Istanbul. If you want some now, you can get it from NaturlisFriend Co:

> **Our company has adopted at the founding of mesir paste and province Manisa and Turkey and mesir paste sought to promote, Mesir paste combining trade, aims to tell everywhere. In specific proportions and certain sequence of 41 kinds of toothpaste Mesir vegetable paste mixed with honey, then become a make occurs by boiling. There are 41 kinds of spices their properties, combined with their own properties, becomes a source of natural power and energy, There is no chemical in the mesir paste, produced manually.**

Meanwhile, on the good ship Venüs in Bodrum, we must be intrigued by a temporary banner attached to a boat proclaiming its role in solid waste collection. But what kind of waste, we ask? Seems like a nice boat. Looks like waste is not a permanent occupation.

As in English, the meaning of a word in Turkish can depend a great deal on the context. Kati, for example, has many meanings including final and rigid. Atik normally means agile, flexible, fit, that sort of thing but, as with cock – a male fowl, a heap of hay, or a method of securing crossing beams by means of a dovetail – so atik can also mean sewage and, collocated with kati, the phrase is inert waste.

Alim is mostly used to imply wisdom and scholarly qualities, but here means uptake or intake. Teknesi means boat and things boat-like. Yariş teknesi is a speedboat, so we can wonder if Toyota's brand-name department knew that.

In all, we have to be glad that the boat's owners have provided a translation. Tourists high on Kaboom, but with only GCSE Turkish, might have gone on board the Venüs expecting something stiff, lissom and intellectual.

# GOOD FOR YOUR BLEEN

Your correspondent often resorts to a cup of the old China, for its cheering and refreshing effects, when several pertinent and depressing answers have occurred to him for that question you see so often in the newspaper ads: Why not be a writer?

Unfortunately, in hope of ameliorating that malady known as writers' bleen, supplies of a particular Yunnan blended tea have not as yet been obtained from the Shining Herb Company of Beijing.

**Orange Puerh Tea has a similar out shape like dry fruits. It was processed by original Xinhui orange from Gaungdong and excellent Puerh Tea from Yunnan in a scientific way. This old orange puerh tea has a special strong flavor, which is like the good old smell only floats in the old time. This tea is good for your bleen and breathing. It also has some therapetutic functions such as draining for increasing spuntum expectoration, relieving cough, refreshing mind, relieving toxication symptoms and diuresis. It will perfectly be your daily health beverage.**

Ah, yes, the good old smell, combined with the increased spuntum – but asking for these qualities in the village shop did not produce a positive response.

# TURDBABY

This Taiwanese manufacturer of novelty mah jongg tiles and monsters is known for the same things that made Muralitheran, Warne, Swann and Laker famous: balls that turn, or niu dan, literally turn egg. These are the equivalent of the Kinder eggs we know, kiddies' treats that unscrew and reveal a toy within. There are vending machines full of them. For egg read baby. For turn, just forget to check the spelling. Simples.

## Pood Till You Drop

Tourists in Talinn hoping to replace nappies or skid-marked nether garments will be disappointed in this pood (shop), which sells items connected with a good night's sleep (und) such as duvet covers and other bed linen in the local tradition. Very nice too.

## Two Fingers To You

Whether or not John Wayne ever ordered two fingers of red-eye in the Last Chance saloon, or the Mexican tequila makers of Los Altos knew that dos dedos was the soldier's farewell, or had seen pictures of Mr Churchill, we remain ignorant.

# *The Bin of Death*

The good folk of Cheshire, whose first instinct on seeing a capacious receptacle will always be to climb into it, are reminded of the potentially fatal consquences of such an action but not really prohibited from it. It leaves a sporting opportunity for bin-explorers. Owners of such bins are recommended to consider plainer language on their signs, for example: If you climb into this bin, you will die. People who produce hazardous wastes, rather than calling our number, will usually tip them on top of you.

NO HAZARDOUS WASTE
NO liquids
NO tyres
NO aerosols
NO oil filters
NO electronic goods
NO asbestos
if you produce these wastes call :-
0870 421 1122

**DANGER**
**DO NOT CLIMB
INTO THE BIN**
It could be emptied at ANY TIME
THE RESULT COULD BE YOUR DEATH!

**SITA**
0870 421 1122
sita co.uk

# *HOUSTON, WE HAVE AN ISSUE.*

In much of this book we have been taking the superpiss out of Johnny Foreigner, but let's not forget our own abuses of our language. Without resting on our laurels, we continue to raise the bar, to quote the blurb from Blue Mango Brasserie in Birmingham, where authenticity forms the very basis of their foundation.

**Bored of sun loungers? Visit Wales.**

**BUPA Help you find healthy.**

These little travesties are deliberate. Help you find healthy? What's that supposed to mean?

Of course, advertising copywriters are more restricted than they used to be. Claims have to be substantiated, which was how one of the best known lines in advertising originated fifty years ago. Nothing acts faster than Anadin, so take nothing. It's faster, as they say, and much cheaper.

Today, we have Domestos – Nothing protects as long. Clears up your everyday issues.

While we try to work out how a bleach clears up issues, we can at least be sure that nothing won't protect us any longer.

Niquitin is slightly cleverer. No other patch is more effective – so don't use nothing, but different brands of patch are just as good.

As they say far away: Vietnam Northern Food Corporation. Not Simply The No. 1. Or, as they almost said in Northern Ireland: The future's bright, the future's protestant loyalist.

Zapata's Mexican Cantina does not sponsor prostitutes at our establishment. If you are a prostitute please refrain from entering our garden or restaurant. If you are unsure whether or not you are a prostitute, please ask one of our friendly security guards to sort it out for you.

感谢合作!
Thanks

por ja multiuso

# McPussy

*máxima limpieza*

## *Silly Fuchs*

If you were having a party in Germany, you might well consider an outside caterer and, provided you were not really interested in a vegetarian option, you could do no better than use Wurst Fuchs of Munich. The company name translates as Sausage Fox, but we must presume they know what they're doing.

# Answers to Spot That Brand

## @ShakyBill
**Noisy:** French butter.
**Shit Begone:** American toilet tissue invented as an art installation by Jed Ela; 100% recycled, dormant at the time of writing.

## @BobLStevo
**Fanny:** Peruvian tinned tuna, also jam.
**Extra Parrot:** Cambodian tea.
**Love Juice:** juice kiosk at Stansted airport.
**McPussy:** Argentinian pan scrubber.

## @Errol_Flynn9
**Flirt:** Belgian nutty chocolate wafer.
**High Gorgeous:** Japanese bread.

**@Marilyn362436**
**Big Nuts:** Belgian chocolate-nut bar.
**Wack Off:** Australian insect repellent.
**Burned Meat:** Chinese biscuits.

**@Errol_Flynn9**
**Wild Drip:** Japanese coffee.
**Soup for Sluts:** Japanese instant pot-noodle.

**@Emperor_Hirohito**
**Eggs of Sacred Crane:** Japanese chocolate (Its taste will probably satisfy you).

**@Tobybelch**
**Nips:** Spanish candy bar.
**Arse:** Chinese notepad.
**Arse:** Austrian energy drink made from Alpine water, vitamins and pomegranite.
**Unbelieveable This is not butter:** Japanese spread.
**Pee:** Ghanaian cola.

# ACKNOWLEDGEMENTS

With many thanks for help to:
Peter Bensimon, Kimberly Brown-Azzarello, Anna-Mei Chadwick, Sui
Chin, Chmee2, Alison Clark, Warwick Faville, Steven Finn, Fvasconcellos,
Jon Goddard, www.historyworld.co.uk, Damian Harte, John Howarth,
Dave Jackson, Nathan Keirn, John Mann, mattspong, Paul Merrill (http://
internationaltoothpastemuseum.blogspot.com), Tina Meyer, John Murphy,
Ali Muskett, Kevin Riley, Scheinwerfermann (en.wikipedia.org/wiki/
User:Scheinwerfermann), Richard Shiner, Bill Shuttle, Suzy Small, Katie
Thorburn, Vinhtantran (en.wikisource.org/wiki/User:Vinhtantran)